Verbs in Action
Fall Down

Dana Meachen Rau

Marshall Cavendish
Benchmark
New York

Can you ice skate? It takes a lot of practice. You might fall. Sometimes it hurts!

Gravity makes you fall. Gravity is a force inside the Earth.

It pulls everything down to the
ground.

Heavy objects make a loud noise when they fall. Light objects might make no sound at all.

What sound does a pot make when it falls? What sound does a feather make?

Objects can break when they fall. A glass breaks into smaller pieces of glass. When an egg falls, it makes a mess.

If you fall, you might break a bone.

A rubber ball does not break when it falls. It bounces!

Bouncing is like falling over and over again.

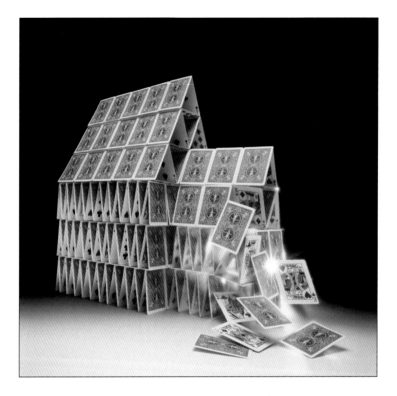

Wind can make things fall. Just one little puff can knock down a house of cards.

The strong winds of a *hurricane* can make a real house fall down.

Loggers make trees fall. They saw down trees for wood to make furniture or paper.

Beavers make trees fall, too.
They use their teeth to cut down
trees to build their homes.

A *waterfall* is a river falling over a cliff. Niagara Falls is a very big waterfall between the United States and Canada.

Rain is another type of falling water. It falls out of clouds in the sky.

Snow is also falling water. Snow is water that is very cold. It is so cold that it freezes.

Snow sometimes falls down the side of a mountain. This is called an *avalanche*.

A skydiver falls from the sky, too. Her *parachute* helps slow her down so she can land safely.

Rocks, called *meteoroids*, fall through outer space. Some fall toward the Earth. People call them shooting stars. Some of these rocks crash onto the ground.

Have you ever been tired running a race? You might "fall behind" the other runners.

You might "fall in love" with
your new pet kitten.

You might "fall to pieces" if you lose your favorite toy.

Most often, falling means something
moves from up to down. Leaves fall
from trees in autumn.

In fact, another name for autumn is fall. It is easy to see why!

Challenge Words

avalanche (AV-uh-lanch)—Snow falling down the side of a
mountain.

gravity (GRAV-i-tee)—A force inside the Earth that pulls
everything down to the ground.

hurricane (HUR-i-kane)—A storm with very strong winds.

loggers (LOG-uhrs)—Workers who cut down trees.

meteoroids (MEE-tee-uhr-oyds)—Falling rocks in space.

parachute (PAR-uh-shoot)—Umbrella-shaped fabric that slows
down a skydiver so she can land safely.

waterfall (WA-tuhr-fall)—A river falling over a cliff.

Index

Page numbers in **boldface** are illustrations.

With thanks to Nanci Vargus, Ed.D. and Beth Walker Gambro, reading consultants

Marshall Cavendish Benchmark
Marshall Cavendish
99 White Plains Road
Tarrytown, New York 10591-9001
www.marshallcavendish.us

Library of Congress Cataloging-in-Publication Data

Rau, Dana Meachen, 1971–
Fall down / by Dana Meachen Rau.
p. cm. — (Bookworms. Verbs in action)
Includes index.
ISBN 0-7614-1936-5
1. Fall (The English word)—Juvenile literature. 2. English language—Verb—Juvenile literature.
I. Title II. Series: Rau, Dana Meachen, 1971- .
Bookworms. Verbs in action.

PE1317.F35R388 2005
428.1—dc22
2004023399

Photo Research by Anne Burns Images

Cover photo: Corbis/Tom & Dee Ann McCarthy

The photographs in this book are used with the permission and through the courtesy of:
Corbis: pp. 1, 12 Myron Jay Dorf; pp. 2, 29 Tom Stewart; p. 4 Paul Barton; p. 7 Randy Faris; pp. 8, 10 Royalty Free;
p. 9 Lew Long; p. 13 Reuters; p. 14 Natalie Fobes; p. 15 Tim Wright; p. 18 Richard Hutchings; p. 19 Galen Rowell; p.
21 W. Wayne Lockwood, M.D.; p. 22 Premium Stock; p. 25 David Pollack; p. 28 Kathleen Brown. SuperStock: p. 5
Anton Vengo; p. 16 Steve Vidler; p. 17 Francisco Cruz; p. 26 Profimedia; p. 27 Lisette Le Bon.

Series design by Becky Terhune

Printed in Malaysia
1 3 5 6 4 2